EYE ON AMERICA

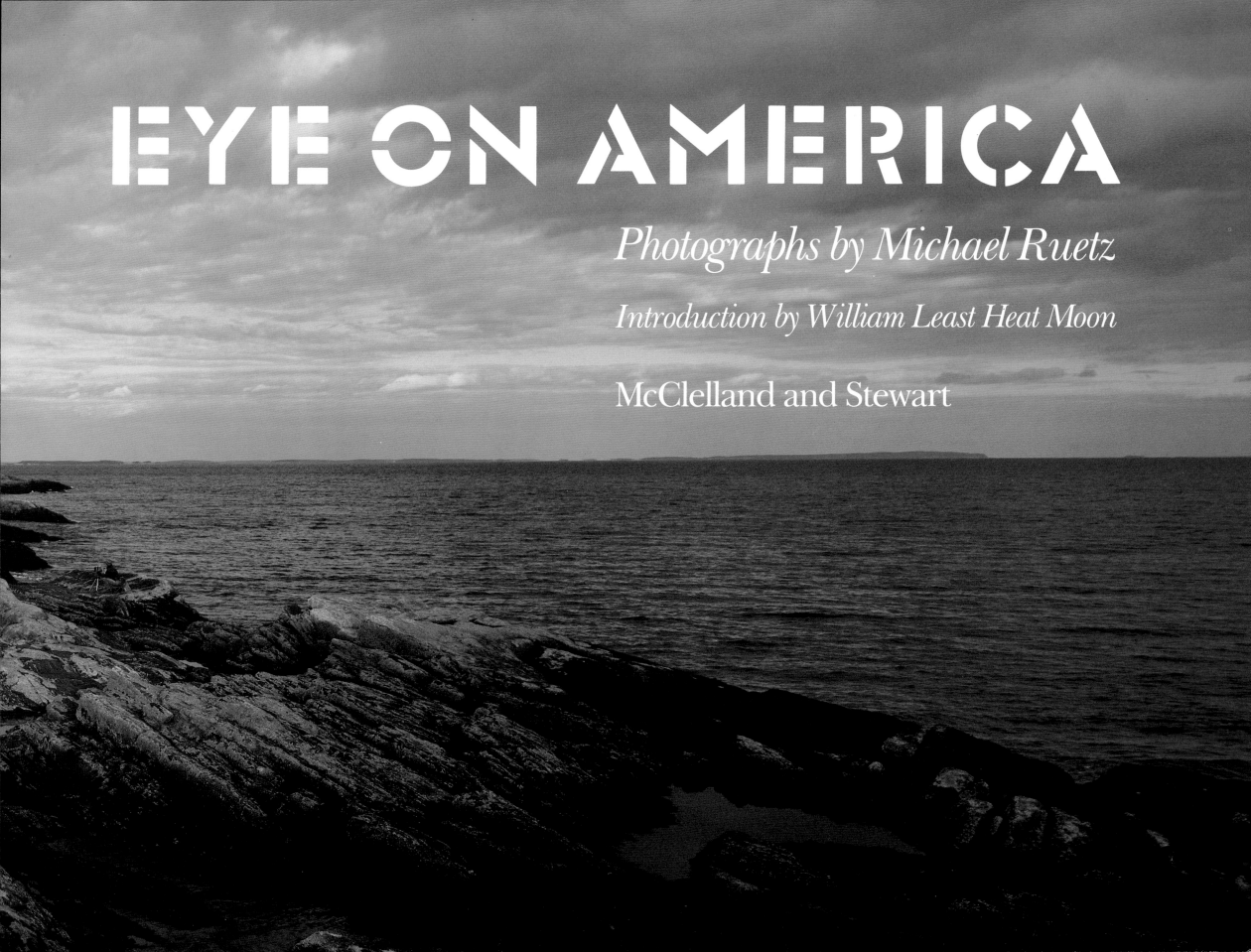

EYE ON AMERICA

Photographs by Michael Ruetz

Introduction by William Least Heat Moon

McClelland and Stewart

To my American friends

Published in Canada by
McClelland and Stewart Limited
The Canadian Publishers
25 Hollinger Road
Toronto, Ontario
M4B 3G2

Canadian Cataloguing in Publication Data

Ruetz, Michael.
    Eye on America

ISBN 0-7710-7866-8
1. United States – Description and travel – 1981-
– Views. I. Title.
E169.04.R83 1984   917.3.'0022'2   C84-098780-3

First edition

First published in the United States of America by New York Graphic Society /
Little, Brown and Company, Boston, in 1984

Frontispiece: Pemaquid, Maine, by Michael Ruetz

Designed by Carl Zahn

Printed in Japan by Dai Nippon Printing Company, Ltd.

Introduction

by William Least Heat Moon

They came so early and so often and they observed so well, they have become more a part of the American past than of the history of their homelands. From their observations came the earliest views of this nation: the logs of Columbus, the account of Thomas Harriot, the watercolors of John White, the drawings of Jacques le Moyne – all of these in the East; and in the West, works like the narratives of Cabeza de Vaca and Francisco Garces.

Except for the English and French, none came to write or paint more frequently than the Teutonic peoples – the Germans and Austrians, the northern Swiss. Many of them we now hardly know: Johann Friedrich Reichel, Gottfried Duden, Bernard Karl, Theodor Griesinger. We know some- what better the artist Karl Bodmer, who accompanied Prince Maximilian on his two-year journey through the West. What John White's luminous watercolors do for eastern history, so Bodmer's do for the West. Americans know their land better because these Europeans came to see and represent.

The tradition continues. In our time the classic photo- graphic odyssey of America is still *The Americans,* by the Swiss- born Robert Frank. But *why* do Europeans still come here to report? Certainly for the oldest reason of the traveler, curios- ity. And, I suspect, for other reasons that even the darkest European notions of contemporary America cannot entirely extinguish. They come because this is yet a place to test a vision or to find a vision, a vision of whatever kind.

If the continentals no longer arrive with the expectation of discovering a pristine land, they nonetheless are happy to find intimations of one in American wilderness or even in the far prospect of cities at night. And if the travelers *know* the United States is a harsh place, they are pleased to discover it also is not. Still, Americans struggle against the European inclination to see this country more as a historical or political concept than as a gathered yet diverse people living on the land. Americans struggle, too, with the Old World propensity to understand the country through only its coastal life. They struggle with the European wish for this nation always to remain a place of expectation, wonder, challenge, hope. And so the Old World continues coming to measure, to define, to compare, to see how its ancestors' dream fares.

Robert Frank, in his journey in 1955–1956, found a peo- ple covered by their own darkness. No reader of his book, surely, can come away from those photographs of turned backs, turned-down mouths, and vacant eyes and feel good about living in this country. Yet Frank helped balance a Euro- pean wish, alive since the Renaissance, to see the New World as a nearly imaginary realm, an Erewhon.

But what the hell? American life is not that unrelievedly bleak and grim. There is fullness and magnificence too. Michael Ruetz, born in 1940 in Berlin, knows the bleak and grim. And that's part of the reason why, when he took to the American road for two years, the eye he turned on America was often that of an earlier European, of one who looks to find the beautiful and mysterious. His eye discloses, in the translated words of the great Oglala medicine man Black Elk, "the beauty and strangeness in the land." To tribal Americans, that perception precedes insight into a larger vision.

When Michael Ruetz was a child, his mother gave him a book of landscape paintings by the German Romantic Caspar David Friedrich. In 1973 Ruetz visited many locations of Friedrich's paintings in Denmark, East Germany, Poland, and Czechoslovakia and photographed them in the emerging and vanishing light that both men love. Almost always in Friedrich's paintings and frequently in Ruetz's photographs, the subject is the light upon the land, in an approach that takes that subject beyond literalness. This book well could have been titled *Light on America.* It is just these fallings and reachings of luminance, natural and otherwise, that reveal the eye Ruetz has on America; if, at times, this eye and these lightings turn the land into an imaginary Renaissance realm, perhaps Americans can use the old vision to reawaken to historical process and to the continuing potential of humankind living in harmony with the land.

You like the abundant display of beauty in these pictures or you don't. But, either way, do not assume that Ruetz was unaware of the ugly. As a photojournalist, he has seen and photographed plenty of it. His emphasis here on magnificence, I think, comes not only from his cultural antecedents but also from his wish to exclude the ephemeral and to emphasize instead the lasting. His logic, in my words, is this: whatever refuse Sophocles and Shakespeare left behind has passed away, and what remains is an inheritance of magnificence. To say that the ugly and worthless, at least in their actuality, are only temporary is a logic of hope. Yet Ruetz did not photograph the beautiful in order to misdirect anyone from the reality of degraded landscapes. He has said, "Seeing beauty makes you want more." These photographs, then, are also a challenge.

At times, Michael Ruetz almost creates this beauty *within* the camera: he catches a casting of light, or he backs away from his subject until the breadth of view minimizes specifics and turns even the jarring details of a city into concordance. With the particular softened, the universal comes forward, and with it, Ruetz hopes, the timeless. In many of his finest images, he has moved back far enough to collect the wide reach of land and city through a camera called the Technorama, a machine well able to capture the awe a European can feel before a land and sky that open out almost beyond imagining. Cityscapes lengthened and distanced become like landscapes – harmonious, eternal, natural.

The struggle of any artist is to find untaken ground. Although panoramic photographs are not new, the recent Technorama has helped Ruetz develop a vision, part Renaissance and part Romantic, into something newer. His hundred-degree sweeps invite the eyes to wander. When landscape photographer Robert Adams said that composition is the lensman's main tool, he was speaking of how it concentrates a viewer's attention. In the Technorama foldouts herein, Ruetz compels attention by expanding the angle of vision. The eyes move and pause and move again. His is a concentration through motion. For a road book, as well as for beings given binocular vision, this is as it should be. These are two-eyed photographs.

Michael Ruetz has another reason for using the wide views of the Technorama: the image produced by this camera metaphorically reflects the course of American history. To speak about the vast human movements into these two billion American acres without using the word *sweep* is difficult. American history, from land-bridge crossings to steamship sailings, is a thing of sweeps. People sweep in, sweep out, sweep on, for better or worse. Maybe it is a Near West parochialism, but to me American history has in it more of the horizontal township and range than the vertical contour and elevation. Just so, the Technorama sweeps the horizon, trimming sky and foreground until the horizontal movement of man across America appears by historical association.

The "highway shots," as Ruetz calls those cramped windshield views between panoramas, give a narrative movement to his journey. Nevertheless, this road book is strangely still. Even with the car lights streaking in and out of Boston and Detroit, these are stopped cities. In town, in the country, these are places just departed. How hard it must have been at times

to empty the scenes. Yet, like Friedrich's Romantic pastorals, as in most landscapes, things are quiet but not dormant. Action impends. Robert Adams once said that "the real job of a landscape painter or photographer [is] to make things stand still." The stillness in these photographs, then, is right.

And that brings me back to Robert Frank. I like to think of *Eye on America* as something of a companion to *The Americans:* both Ruetz and Frank were raised in a Germanic culture, both traveled the United States for two years, both photographed the same number of states, both emphasized the coasts (especially California), and both selected a nearly identical number of pictures for publication. With that, the differences take over. *The Americans,* while almost lightless, is a passionate book of movement and chaos—tilted horizons, blurred images, harried faces. It is full of the vacancy of an empty people.

None of these things is in *Eye on America.* Here the photographs, in their stillness, are without people yet charged with them; Ruetz knows that the jumped hare's presence is sometimes more poignant from the impression in the grass where it has lain. His photographs show a land that is open not because it is vacant but because it is expansive. And if the people are still harried, as in Frank's depiction, here they seem only to have gone aside momentarily for rest. These two European views in combination, my guess is, reveal a more complete representation of life in this land.

Author's Note

The overwhelming majority of us own a camera. We use it to record our visual memories. The results are as varied in quality as they are in subject matter. After a decade or more, we decide to paste them into an album; we give them a certain organization or system and frequently a different chronology; we leave out some and wish we had taken others. If, however, we conceive of a project in which the individual pieces are to have some kind of relationship to the whole, then our efforts will change direction and our results will turn out differently; we will preselect certain persons, places, things, and events, and "shoot" them. The choice we make of camera, film, lens, focal length, aperture, exposure time, and many other variables will be determined well in advance. We are aiming at more than the mere sum of the parts.

Eye on America was intended as a book from the very outset. The photographic book has become a medium in its own right in the fifteen-odd decades that have elapsed since the invention of photography, although the results of Louis Nicéphore Niépce and Louis Daguerre bear as much resemblance to the photographs of Walker Evans as Gutenberg's Bible does to *Life* magazine. The development of the photographic book has taken place in the century or so since the introduction of the halftone printing plate that sent the woodcut, lithograph, and heliogravure the way of the village smithy. New and advanced printing techniques and papers have created possibilities of which our precursors didn't dare to dream.

Photograph by Yuriy Bihun

My problem was to compress the vastness of America into a single, albeit voluminous, book. Developing an approach to such an enormous subject as America presented a special and difficult challenge, particularly to a German photographer. For previous books I had relied upon the habit or method of drawing up lists of specific sites and itineraries, to which I scrupulously adhered – well, more or less. However, it seemed to me that America required a different approach. I therefore abandoned my old method and ventured into a kind of odyssey without limits in time or space. I took up residence in the United States, worked out of rented cars, and drove an average of 130 miles per day over a period of two years. I traveled at off-season times that allowed me to be alone with the subject that I was photographing. Never did I intend to produce a geographically all-encompassing portrait of America; more ambitious photographers than I have failed. My simple aim was to see what would result when I let America itself serve as a spark to ignite my photographic imagination.

In terms of land and population, the United States is one of the biggest countries on earth. How is it, then, that so few Americans are to be seen in my *Eye on America*? How is it possible to ignore the ubiquitous mass events, the rodeos, stock-car races, conventions, demonstrations, marches on Washington, rocket launchings, and football games, to decline pointing my lens at the easy-living, outgoing, generous, and gregarious American people? I can only answer that I feel that the task of photographing Americans in a knowing, perceptive, and con-

vincing way is best left to American photographers. Moreover, extensive stretches of America are sparsely populated and much of the landscape has not fallen prey to the "bigger-is-better" of city builders. It is possible to find as much solitude in America as in the Antarctic, and solitude is what I need in order to make meaningful pictures. Indeed, I consider my ability to endure long periods of solitude, not seeing anybody, not speaking with anybody, essential to my work and my results. The reader will therefore find that I have limited my picture-taking to landscape and cityscape, wilderness and metropolis.

Not that I have neglected the men and women of America; although they are rarely to be seen in an image, they are almost always there through the traces of their endeavors: in a boat landing, or a footpath, a corral fence, or just an asphalt road. After all, man is the measure of all things, and it is only possible for us to measure the magnitude and the territorial expanse of America by relating them to human dimensions; mankind itself determines the size of its creations.

Visual recording always involves a trade-off; one attains a certain quality of freedom only in return for giving up another. All photographs result from the inseparable bond with subjects that exist in the here and now. No photograph can be made from memory as a painting can be. No photographer could be present at the ceremony of Napoleon crowning himself emperor, so Jacques Louis David's painting must serve for all time. On the other hand, no painting of the burning of

Atlanta has the immediacy of Mathew Brady's incomparable photographs of the American Civil War. Being in the right place at the right time with the right equipment cannot be overestimated, nor can it be denied that a certain amount of luck is indispensable. This portrait of America developed out of rambling and instinctive meanderings; to say I had a plan would be saying too little, to say I had a program would be saying too much.

When taking photographs, I like to feel that I am recording more than just a visual instant of some mountain, lake, or wheat field. Light – and in mechanical terms photography is nothing more than recording light – has interested me from the time I first set my eyes on the paintings of Caspar David Friedrich, the great north-German Romantic. In perhaps more than half of the photographs in this book, I am more concerned with showing light than objects; the objects are only vehicles with which light is connected. My busiest hours were those just before sunrise and after sunset. My work often started in the dead of the night when I drove out to reach a destination in time. Monument Valley, for example, I was able to photograph at sunrise and twilight, thus creating a pair of pictures of which I had always dreamed. As America has more artificial illumination than any other place in the world, I frequently made use of the peculiar situation that occurs when artificial light and natural light reach a balance. The light of day dwindles and the neon signs start to bloom like the moon cactus. It was at such moments that I found my stride.

I rarely lingered at one place for a long time; there is a point at which all the waiting in the world will not suffice or bring the desired result. One rare exception occurred while I was working on the closing image, HAVE A NICE DAY. I took several days on this one shot, because I was interested in achieving a certain ironic and eerie quality. While I was waiting and working, the signpost was slinging words like CASH, NOW, DON'T SMOKE, and NATURAL at me.

Because of the enormous distances, America has been on wheels ever since the early pioneers set out cross-country in their prairie schooners. Ever since the days of Henry Ford, and thanks to the ingenuity of the Detroit automobile makers, Americans have spent a large part of their waking day behind the wheel of a car. It seemed important to me to show America exactly that way. For that purpose, I used three motorized Leicas and took thousands of photographs through the windshield of my rented car.

During these two years, I tried to look as little as possible into the older photographic books; I was trying to keep my mind clear of the impressive work of the great American photographers. There are, however, several images deliberately created as *hommages* to Ansel Adams, Edward Weston, and Walker Evans – masters to whom we all owe very much.

That America has its seamy sides, its slums and trash heaps, its decaying cities and junkyards and noxious fumes and polluted rivers, is something that cannot be denied. None of this has escaped the attention of photographers. Although this book clearly treats the ironies as well as the magnificence of America, I chose not to dwell on its ugliness. In the first place, Lewis Hine, Arthur Rothstein, Walker Evans, and Dorothea Lange have captured the American shadows better than any photographers prior or subsequent. They were—quite legitimately—concerned with improving the quality of American life, tuning up the performance to match better with the American promise. Their photographic diagnoses jolted Americans into repairing the major ills of their society. They also found disciples and, unfortunately, imitators, who make a profession out of self-righteousness. Ansel Adams has called our attention to this preoccupation, this fascination with the corrupt and spoiled in America that has become something of a fashion: "It seems 'correct' to see America's slums and highways this way. There is little joy and no love left; mostly pollution, ugliness and depression. We know there is more." I share Adams's desire to seek these other sides of the country. Perhaps I should put it this way: I try to show what can and must be appreciated in America, while photographers like Lewis Hine tried to provoke Americans into correcting ills and injustices. "My" America is one I would not like to see "corrected."

* * *

Walker Evans was once asked about the cameras, films, and so forth, that he employed. His reply was that the inquirer should ask the poet about the typewriter he used. Perhaps he was responding out of resentment at such an obtrusive question, or in irritation at the naive assumption that the camera and not the photographer is responsible for good pictures. Of course, if only the camera were required, one photo taken with a Leica would be as good as the next. In fact, Evans was merely calling our attention to the fact that the person behind the camera is decisive. Nevertheless, I place enormous value on, and confidence in, the tools of my trade. Only certain kinds of tools can be used to mediate between me and my subject; it is important that I choose the right ones.

For the single-page images that are reproduced here, I used an assortment of Leica and Leicaflex cameras with lenses ranging from 15 to 800 millimeters. I am so familiar with these tools that they feel like a pen in my hand. I use them almost instinctively, without second thoughts.

The double-page spreads and foldouts were all made with a Technorama camera built by the Munich company Linhof. Whereas conventional 35-millimeter cameras have lenses that produce an image with a height-to-width ratio of 3:4, the Technorama combines two such images side by side, resulting in an overall height-to-width ratio of 1:3. The original transparency measures 57 by 180 millimeters. The effect is almost that of a panoramic view, because there are about one hundred degrees of vision registered on the film, but unlike a panoramic camera, the Technorama has a fixed lens, rather than one that swings from left to right. The Technorama looks at the world the way we do.

It is an extremely straight camera, perfect for documentation. A vertical thread that I placed over the center of the viewfinder allows me to compose photographs with two halves of equal weight, thereby helping me to avoid losing elements of the picture in the book's centerfold—a problem that photographic books often suffer from. With a few exceptions, it has not yet been used for fine photography, and its artistic potential has yet to be explored.

For all my pictures I used Kodak films, which I consider to be the best: Ektachrome film with the Technorama, Kodachrome for those photographs made with the Leicas. Some of these pictures are proof that the best lenses in the world are still produced by Leitz. I was also equipped with a number of special filters made by a small but very innovative manufacturer in Bavaria: Mr. Martin Summer. Some of these filters were made to my specifications.

The Technorama camera, in particular, offers many possibilities with which I have only now become wholly familiar. It has changed my way of perceiving and photographing, and has become indispensable to me. No camera could be better suited to convey the vastness of the American continent.

Acknowledgments

It would be presumptuous to pretend that this book was the result of my efforts alone. For their help and encouragement I would like to thank: Michael S. Cullen, Angela Siemonsen, Ingrid T. Schick, Rita and St. Clair A. Sullivan, Petra E. Benteler, Mr. and Mrs. Alvin B. Krongard, Peter Range, Marita Kankowski, Margot Klingsporn, Yuriy and Irene Bihun, Helmuth Penzlien, and many others. My special expression of thanks goes to Terry Reece Hackford and the staff of New York Graphic Society Books / Little, Brown and Company and to Carl Zahn for their understanding and for helping to create a book out of these photographs, and to William Least Heat Moon, in whose *Blue Highways* I later reexperienced much of what I had felt and reflected upon during my American journey.

Michael Ruetz

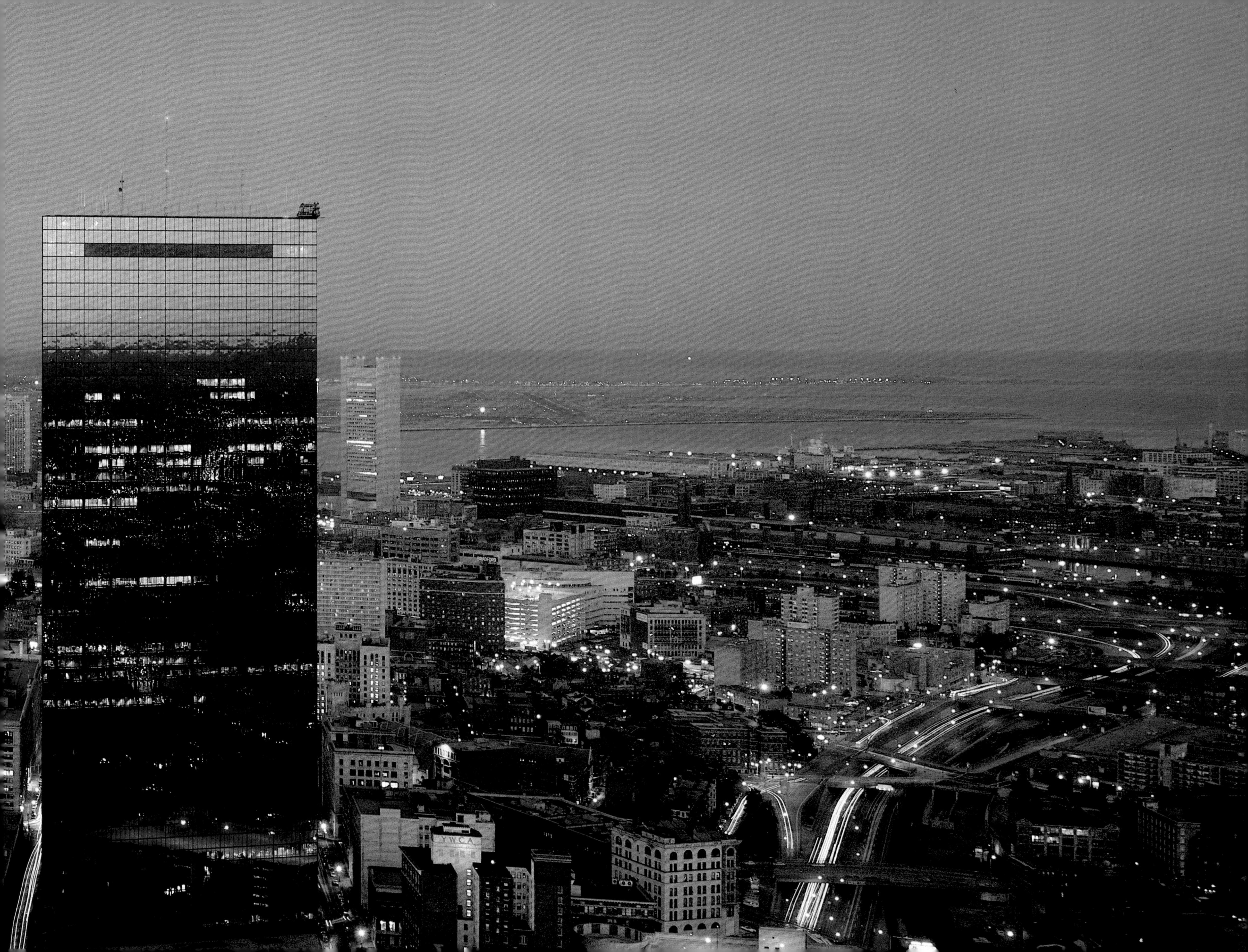
BRADFORD
YWCA

List of Plates